D0712283

Railway Series, No. 16

BRANCH LINE ENGINES

by
THE REV. W. AWDRY

with illustrations by
JOHN T. KENNEY

HEINEMANN · LONDON

William Heinemann Ltd
Michelin House
81 Fulham Road
London SW3 6RB

LONDON MELBOURNE AUCKLAND

First published in 1961 by Edmund Ward
Reprinted 1989 by William Heinemann Ltd
Copyright © 1961 William Heinemann Ltd
All rights reserved

ISBN 0 434 92793 7

Printed and bound in Great Britain by
William Clowes Limited, Beccles and London

Foreword

DEAR FRIENDS,

We never have a dull moment on our Branch Line. Thomas was silly and got into trouble, so a Diesel Rail-car called Daisy came. She caused trouble, but has now promised to be good, so the Fat Controller has kindly given her another chance.

Meanwhile Toby chased a bull, Percy got into a predicament and . . . .

But you must read the stories for yourselves.

THE AUTHOR

Thomas Comes to Breakfast

THOMAS the Tank Engine has worked his Branch Line for many years. "You know just where to stop, Thomas!" laughed his Driver. "You could almost manage without me!"

Thomas had become conceited. He didn't realise his Driver was joking. "Driver says I don't need him now," he told the others.

"Don't be so daft!" snorted Percy.

"I'd never go without *my* Driver," said Toby earnestly. "I'd be frightened."

"Pooh!" boasted Thomas. "I'm not scared."

"You'd never dare!"

"I would then. You'll see!"

It was dark next morning when the Fire-lighter came. Thomas drowsed comfortably as the warmth spread through his boiler. He woke again in daylight. Percy and Toby were still asleep. Thomas suddenly remembered. "Silly stick-in-the-muds," he chuckled. "I'll show them! Driver hasn't come yet, so here goes."

He cautiously tried first one piston, then the other. "They're moving! They're moving!" he whispered. "I'll just go out, then I'll stop and 'wheeeeesh'. That'll make them jump!"

Very, very quietly he headed for the door.

Thomas thought he was being clever; but really he was only moving because a careless cleaner had meddled with his controls. He soon found his mistake.

He tried to "wheeeeesh", but he couldn't. He tried to stop, but he couldn't. He just kept rolling along.

"The buffers will stop me," he thought hopefully, but that siding had no buffers. It just ended at the road.

Thomas's wheels left the rails and crunched the tarmac. "Horrors!" he exclaimed, and shut his eyes. He didn't dare look at what was coming next.

8

The Station-master's family were having breakfast. They were eating ham and eggs.

There was a crash—the house rocked—broken glass tinkled—plaster peppered their plates.

Thomas had collected a bush on his travels. He peered anxiously into the room through its leaves. He couldn't speak. The Station-master grimly strode out and shut off steam.

His wife picked up her plate. "You miserable engine," she scolded. "Just look what you've done to our breakfast! Now I shall have to cook some more." She banged the door. More plaster fell. This time, it fell on Thomas.

Thomas felt depressed. The plaster was tickly. He wanted to sneeze, but he didn't dare in case the house fell on him. Nobody came for a long time. Everyone was much too busy.

At last workmen propped up the house with strong poles. They laid rails through the garden, and Donald and Douglas, puffing hard, managed to haul Thomas back to the Yard.

His funnel was bent. Bits of fencing, the bush, and a broken window-frame festooned his front, which was badly twisted. He looked comic.

The Twins laughed and left him. He was in disgrace.

"You are a very naughty engine."

"I know, Sir. I'm sorry, Sir." Thomas's voice was muffled behind his bush.

"You must go to the Works, and have your front end mended. It will be a long job."

"Yes, Sir," faltered Thomas.

"Meanwhile," said the Fat Controller, "a Diesel Rail-car will do your work."

"A D-D-Diesel, Sir?" Thomas spluttered.

"Yes, Thomas. Diesels *always* stay in their sheds till they are wanted. Diesels *never* gallivant off to breakfast in Station-masters' houses." The Fat Controller turned on his heel, and sternly walked away.

Daisy

THE Fat Controller stood on the platform. Percy and Toby watched him anxiously. "Here," he said, "is Daisy, the Diesel Rail-car who has come to help while Thomas is—er—indisposed."

"Please, Sir," asked Percy, "will she go, Sir, when Thomas comes back, Sir?"

"That depends," said the Fat Controller. "Meanwhile, however long she stays, I hope you will both make her welcome and comfortable."

"Yes, Sir, we'll try, Sir," said the engines.

"Good. Run along now, and show her the shed. She will want to rest after her journey."

Daisy was hard to please. She shuddered at the Engine Shed. "This is dreadfully smelly," she announced. "I'm highly sprung, and anything smelly is bad for my swerves."

They tried the Carriage Shed. "This is better," said Daisy, "but whatever is that rubbish?"

The "rubbish" turned out to be Annie, Clarabel, and Henrietta, who were most offended.

"We won't stay to be insulted," they fumed. Percy and Toby had to take them away, and spend half the night soothing their hurt feelings.

The engines woke next morning feeling exhausted.

Daisy, on the other hand, felt bright and cheerful. "Uu-ooo! Uu-ooo!" she tooted as she came out of the Yard, and backed to the Station.

"Look at me!" she purred to the waiting Passengers. "I'm the latest Diesel, highly sprung and right up to date. You won't want Thomas's bumpy old Annie and Clarabel now."

The Passengers were interested. They climbed in and sat back comfortably, waiting for Daisy to start.

Every morning a Van is coupled to Thomas's first train. The Farmers send their milk to the Station, and Thomas takes it down to the Dairy.

Thomas never minds the extra load, but Daisy did. As soon as she saw that the Van was to be coupled to her, she stopped purring. "Do they expect me to pull that?" she asked indignantly.

"Surely," said her Driver, "you can pull one Van."

"I won't," said Daisy. "Percy can do it. He loves messing about with trucks."

She began to shudder violently.

"Nonsense," said her Driver. "Come on now, back down."

Daisy lurched backwards. She was so cross that she blew a fuse. "Told you," she said, and stopped.

The Shunter, the Guard, the Station-master, and her Driver all argued with her, but it was no use.

"It's Fitter's orders," she said.

"What is?"

"My Fitter's a very nice man. He is interested in my case. He comes every week, and examines me carefully. 'Daisy,' he says, 'never, never pull. You're highly sprung, and pulling is bad for your swerves.'

"So that's how it is," finished Daisy.

"Stuff and nonsense!" said the Station-master.

"I can't understand," said the Shunter, "whatever made the Fat Controller send us such a feeble...."

"F-f-f-feeble!" spluttered Daisy. "Let me...."

"Stop arguing," grumbled the Passengers. "We're late already."

So they uncoupled the Van, and Daisy purred away feeling very pleased with herself. "That's a good story," she chuckled. "I'll do just what work I choose and no more."

But she said it to herself.

Bull's-eyes

TOBY the Tram Engine has cowcatchers and sideplates. They help to prevent animals getting hurt if they stray on to the line. Daisy thought they were silly. She said Toby was afraid of getting hurt himself.

"I'm not," said Toby indignantly.

"You are. *I've* not got stupid cowcatchers, but *I'm* not frightened. I'd just toot, and they'd all get out of the way."

"But they don't," said Toby simply.

"They would with me. Animals *always* run if you toot and look them in the eye."

"Even bulls?"

"Even bulls," said Daisy confidently.

Daisy had never met a bull, but she purred away quite unconcerned. At the level-crossing cars waited behind gates to let her pass. She tooted at a farm-crossing, and a horse and cart halted while she went by.

"Pooh!" she said. "It's easy. I just toot, and they all stand aside. Poor little Toby! I *am* sorry he's frightened."

At the next Station, a Policeman was waiting. "There's a bull on the line," he warned them. "Please drive it along towards the Farmer."

Daisy was excited. "Now," she thought, "I'll show Toby how to manage bulls."

Champion wasn't really a fierce bull, but this morning he was cross. They had driven him away before he had finished breakfast, and tried to put him in a cattle-float. They had pulled him and pushed him, prodded and slapped him, but he wouldn't go.

He broke away, and trotted down the road. He saw a fence, jumped it, and slithered down a slope.

Champion was surprised. This was a new kind of field. It had a brown track at the bottom, but there was plenty of grass on each side, and he was still hungry.

"Uuuu Oooo!" tooted Daisy. "Go on!"

Champion had his back to her. He was too busy to pay any attention.

"Uuuuuuu Ooooooo!" said Daisy again.

Champion went on eating.

"This is all wrong," thought Daisy. "How can I look him in the eye if he won't turn round? Uuuuuuuuuu Ooooooooooo!"

At last Champion turned and noticed Daisy. "Moooooooo!" he said, and came towards her, still chewing. He wondered what she was.

"Uuu Ooo!" said Daisy feebly. "Why doesn't he run away?"

The Guard and the Policeman tried to "shoo" Champion. But he wouldn't stay "shooed". As soon as they turned away, he came back. He was a most inquisitive animal.

"Go on, Daisy," said her Driver. "He's harmless."

"Yes," said Daisy unhappily. "*You* know he's harmless, and *I* know he's harmless, but does *he* know? Besides, look at his horns. If I bumped into him he might hurt—er—them. The Farmer wouldn't like that."

Champion came close, and sniffed at Daisy. "Oooof," she said, backing hastily.

Toby was surprised to find Daisy back once more at the Station. The Passengers told him about the bull. He chuckled.

"Bulls *always* run if you toot and look them in the eye. Eh Daisy?"

Daisy said nothing.

"Ah well!" Toby went on. "We live and learn. I'd better chase him for you, I suppose."

He clanked away.

But Champion took no notice of Toby's bell or whistle. He didn't move till Toby "hooshed" him with steam. Then Toby gently "shooed" him along the track to where the Farmer and his men were waiting.

Daisy had an exhausting day. Toby and Percy often met her on their journeys, and though they never mentioned bulls, they gave her pitying looks. It made her so cross!

Her last journey ended at the Top Station. Some boys were on the platform. Suddenly one of them came running, holding a paper bag. "Look!" he shouted. "I've got a quarter of bull's-eyes. I think they're super, don't you?"

They shared the sweets and sucked happily.

"Grrrrrh!" said Daisy. "Keep your old bull's-eyes." She scuttled to her shed.

Percy's Predicament

TOBY brought Henrietta to the Top Station.
Percy was grumpily shunting. "Hullo,
Percy," he said, "I see Daisy's left the milk
again."

"I'll have to make a special journey with it,
I suppose," grumbled Percy. "Anyone would
think I'd nothing to do."

Toby pondered the problem. "Tell you
what," he said at last, "I'll take the milk; you
fetch my trucks."

Their Drivers and the Station-master agreed,
and both engines set off. They thought it would
be a nice change.

Percy trundled away to the quarry. He had never been there before. "It's steep," he thought, "but I can manage. Trucks don't dare to play tricks on me now."

He marshalled them in a lordly way. "Hurry along there," he said, and bumped them if they dallied. The trucks were annoyed.

"This is Toby's place," they grumbled, "Percy's got no right to poke his funnel up here and push us around."

They whispered and passed the word.

"Pay Percy out!"

At last they were all arranged. "Come along," puffed Percy sharply. "No nonsense."

"We'll give him nonsense!" giggled the trucks, but they followed so quietly that Percy thought they were completely under control.

They rumbled along the twisty line till they saw ahead the notice saying ALL TRAINS STOP TO PIN DOWN BRAKES.

"Peep! Peep! Peep!" whistled Percy. "Brakes, Guard, please!" But before he could check them the trucks surged forward. "On! On!" they cried.

Percy, taken by surprise, could not stop them, and in a moment they were careering down the hill.

"Help! Help!" whistled Percy. The man on duty at the street-crossing rushed to warn traffic with his red flag, but was too late to switch Percy to the "runaway" siding.

A slow-moving cockerel lost his tail feathers as Percy thundered across, but Percy couldn't bother with him. He had other things to worry about.

Frantically trying to grip the rails, he slid past the Engine Shed into the Yard. "Peeep peeeeeeeep! Look out!" he whistled. His Driver and Fireman jumped clear. Percy shut his eyes and waited for the end.

At the end of the Yard there are sheds where workmen shape rough stone brought from the quarry. Then they load it into trucks, which are pulled to another siding out of the way. A train of these stood here when Percy came slithering down.

The Guard had left his Van. He was talking to the Station-master. They heard frantic whistling and a splintering crash. They rushed from the office.

The Brakevan was in smithereens. Percy, still whistling fit to burst, was perched on a couple of trucks, while his own trucks were piled up behind him.

The Fat Controller arrived next day. Toby and Daisy had helped to remove most of the wreckage, but Percy still stood on his perch.

"We must now try," said the Fat Controller crossly, "to run the Branch Line with Toby and a Diesel. You have put us in an Awkward Predicament."

"I'm sorry, Sir."

"You can stay there," the Fat Controller went on, "till we are ready. Perhaps it will teach you to be careful with trucks."

Percy sighed. The trucks wobbled beneath his wheels. He quite understood about awkward predicaments.

The Fat Controller spoke severely to Daisy, too. "My engines do not tell lies," he said. "They work hard, with no shirking. I send lazy engines away."

Daisy was ashamed.

"However," he went on, "Toby says you worked hard yesterday after Percy's accident, so you shall have another chance."

"Thank you, Sir," said Daisy. "I *will* work hard, Sir. Toby says he'll help me."

"Excellent! What Toby doesn't know about Branch Line problems," the Fat Controller chuckled, "such as—er—bulls, isn't worth knowing. Our Toby's an Experienced Engine."

Thomas came back next day, and Percy was sent to be mended. Annie and Clarabel were delighted to see Thomas again, and he took them for a run at once because they hadn't been out while he was away.

Thomas, Toby, and Daisy are now all friends. Daisy often takes the milk for Thomas, and when Toby is busy, she takes Henrietta.

Toby has taught Daisy a great deal. She "shooed" a cow off the line all by herself the other day!

That shows you, doesn't it?